WHISPERS AND SHADOWS

WHISPERS AND SHADOWS

A Poetic Voyage of the Heart and Soul

AMY LEE

Amy Lee
Whispers and Shadows
A Poetic Voyage of the Heart and Soul

Published by Spines Publishing Platform
ISBN: 979-8-89691-595-9

CONTENTS

Part Three
SEASONS OF CHANGE (20 POEMS)

Part One

WHISPERS OF THE HEART (20 POEMS)

Theme: Love, connection, and longing.

Introduction: Reflecting on love in its many forms—romantic, platonic, familial, and the quiet moments that fill the heart.

ETERNAL GLOW

Each passerby slips into the fog of my mind,
But your memory lingers, steadfast, refined.
Through crowded streets, faces dim and recede,
Yet your glow remains, the one light I need.
Night after night, you visit my dreams,
A quiet beacon, weaving luminous streams.
You are the constant, where all else redeems.

A JOURNEY TO YOU

I have walked every road in this world, so wide,
Through mountains and valleys where dreams reside.
Against the currents of time, I stride,
For a moment when our fates collide,
To find you, my love, by my side.

Having given it to you,
I expect nothing in return.
If you are at the lake, I'll be the shore.
If the mountain, I'll be the grass that adorns your
     beauty.

A GIFT IN THE SNOW

I sent a message through the earthly plain,
Carried by winds and winter's refrain.
Inviting the snow to fall softly,
A gift for you, my love, my all.
In its whispers, hear my call.

THE PRICE OF LOVE

I love you, darling, with all my heart,
Even if you feel just a fraction, a part.
No regrets for the sacrifices I made,
Your happiness is the price I've gladly paid.

ETERNAL WHISPERS

In the vast expanse where galaxies shine,
Two stars connect, their fates align.
Though millions of years may come and go,
Their whispers of love continue to flow.
Time stretches thin, but their hearts remain,
A bond unbroken by distance or strain.
One word, "same," echoes, steadfast and true,
A timeless promise in the cosmic hue.

BESIDE ME ALWAYS

I want you close, in every way,
Beside me, with me, night and day.
Our hands entwined, your warmth so near
As I softly whisper, "I love you, my dear."

GUARDIANS OF LIGHT

Yes, you are the Sun, and I'm the Moon,
Our rhythm dances to a timeless tune.
If the Earth spins beneath our light,
Together we'll guard it, day and night.

FLAME OF LOVE

What is love, I ask the skies,
A bond where life and death entwine.
A flame that burns, yet never dies,
A truth no words could define,
A vow that lives beyond all time.

FRAGRANCE OF LONGING

Flower, if you wish to bloom, then bloom,
Though you may not want to, still you do.
I hold back from seeing you, yet think of you still-
Your fragrance fills my heart, a longing I can't kill.

UNSTOPPABLE LOVE

The clouds drift freely across the sky,
As trees bend low when the winds rush by.
No force can halt the heart's deep ache,
Not even gods the bonds can break.
For love will find the path it must take.

CRESCENT PROMISE

In the night, the new moon's gentle curve,
A fleeting glance, a promise we preserve.
When the crescent hooks the sky's embrace,
We'll meet again, in love's own sacred space.

BLOSSOMS IN MOONLIGHT

The spring moon holds tender grace,
Its light still lingers in a soft embrace.
For separate apart, it shines so bright,
Illuminating blossoms at night.
Though flowers fall, their glow remains,
A solace for lovers in their pains.

THE UNIVERSE'S GLOW

You are unlike anyone else, for I love you so,
I've always believed you hold the universe's glow.
With flowers of joy, I'll gather them nearby,
And fruits of beauty, my love, I'll bring here.
Kisses for all seasons, tender and true,
Like a spring breeze, I'll cherish you.

IN THE WINDS OF FUJI

On Mount Fuji, where the heavens kiss the sky,
A love was born that could never die.
Like the mountain's peak, so strong and true,
Their hearts united as if they knew the world.
In every whisper of the wind, their love will lie.

IN EVERY WAY

I want to tell you, from deep inside,
You came unbidden yet filled the void wide.
Now you're the heart of my every day,
I love you, forever, in every way.

SHAPED IN LOVE

You love me, I love you,
A bond so deep, tender, and true.
Like fire, our passion burns ever bright,
Two lumps of clay, shaped in love's light.
In my clay, your essence will stay,
In life and in death, we are one always.

TIMELESS REUNION

Meeting you feels like an old friend's return,
A gentle warmth, familiar and stern.
We share a smile on paths entwined,
While worlds around us fade in kind.
The stars, the moon, like dust drift by—
Yet here we stand, both you and I.

THROUGH SNOW AND TIME

If, in the future, we walk through the snow together,
Hand in hand, we'll weather the years that pass.
This life is already one spent growing old side by side,
No wind, no frost can change the joy in our hearts.

MELODY OF THE NIGHT

Walked beneath a sky of stars,
City lights fading far. In night's quiet,
I heard the trees sigh,
A soft melody stirring my heart's reply.
Lost in the crowd, yet lifted high—
Dreams, love, and faith in my endless sky.

Part Two

SHADOWS OF LOSS (20 POEMS)

Theme: Grief, separation, and the ache of what has been lost.

Introduction: Exploring the tender pain of good-byes, the emptiness of longing, and the process of healing.

ECHOES

The room still speaks your name,
a whisper in the dust.
I reach for the shadow of you—
but it scatters,
as if even memory
can't bear my touch.

EMPTY CHAIR

Your place at the table
still waits for you,
A silent witness
laughter turned hollow.
The scrape of chairs,
the clink of glasses-
Nothing fills the space
you've left behind.

___

FIRST FROST

___

Winter crept in
the day you left.
Even now,
when spring returns,
the ice in my chest
Refusal to thaw.

ASHES

You were here,
and now you are not.
All I have left
are the ashes of you—
fine dust slipping
through my fingers,
ungraspable,
like time.

A LETTER TO THE UNANSWERED

I'm writing to you,
though you'll never reply.
My words fall into silence—
a void too vast to fill.
Still, I press pen to paper,
as if I could summon you
back into this world.

THE WEIGHT OF ABSENCE

Your absence has a weight–
heavier than your presence ever was.
It drapes across my shoulders,
a burden I carry
with each faltering step forward.

SEALED PHOTOGRAPH

A smile caught in a frame,
preserved but lifeless.
I don't open it often–
the ache of what's frozen there
cuts deeper than I dare admit.

MIDNIGHT CONVERSATIONS

At night,
I still speak to you
in the darkness.
The silence answers back,
its edges soft,
almost like your voice.

WAVES OF YOU

Grief is the ocean.
Some days,
It's a ripple—
a gentle ache.
Other days,
It's a storm—
and I am drowning.

WHAT REMAINS

You are gone.
But you left pieces of you
tucked into corners of me—
your laugh in my dreams,
your words in my heart.
You are gone,
but not lost.

THE LAST GOODBYE

Healing begins
not when the pain ends,
but when I learn
to carry it gently-
A fragile thing
I no longer fear.

THE PATH THAT LED ME

I remember flowers blooming on green trees,
But did I feel the chill of an empty night?
Most unforgettable is the path that led me here,
Once upright and strong, now seeking who'll share joy
   and sorrow.

SILENT SCARS

The human heart, a quiet, shadowed space,
Where echoes linger, time can't erase.
Wounds of youth leave their silent trace,
Soft scars hidden yet tied in place.
Though years may pass, and laughter bloom,
Some aches dwell deep, a constant gloom.

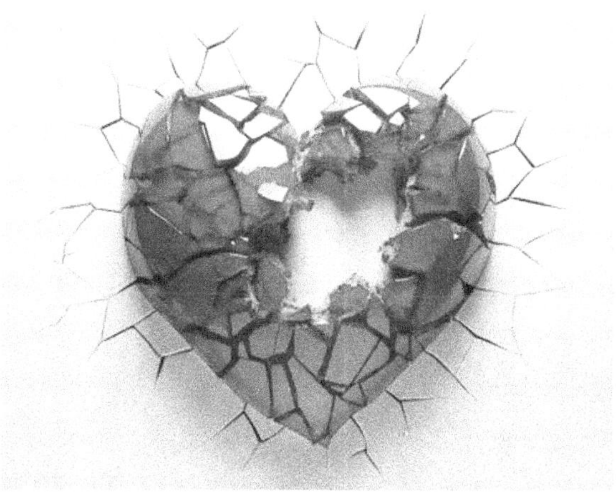

THE UNCHANGED PATH

I had hoped this journey was far away
Would help me forget your beautiful eyes,
To sever the lingering feelings
And the sorrows that even autumn winds can't
    shake off.
Who would have thought, in the end,
The mountains and rivers remain the same,
And love remains unchanged.
Your figure
Just behind me, then suddenly ahead again.

THE ECHO OF LONGING

Remember the grace of our first meeting,
Countless nights of longing, hearts fleeting.
Time flows swiftly, leaving dismay,
Years lost in love's lonely sway.
A quiet ache that won't fade away.

ASHES OF LONGING

Quietly anxious, sickly and weak,
Tossing and turning through sleepless nights.
Inch by inch, longing has turned to ashes,
Desiring to be close to the fragrant dew, yet always
out of reach.

WATER INTO TEARS

If there truly were a kind of water
That could let you and me drink without getting
*   drunk,*
Then perhaps there is a kind of tear
That could let you and me shed without sorrow.
Always seeing love as too perfect,
That feeling of gambling at everything,
In this life losing the promises of past lives,
Only then did we realize that water had quietly
*   turned into tears.*

WHISPERS ON THE BRIDGE

Once parted on the bridge so fair,
I linger in the silent air.
Each whispered breeze, a haunting sigh,
Still hoping for your voice nearby.

UNSPOKEN DISTANCE

In the quiet shadows, let us stay unseen,
Where I want to meet is but a distant dream.
For in the unknown, love cannot begin,
No heartache stirs, no pain within.
Let us remain as strangers, apart,
Where our paths diverge, no need for a start.
To keep our hearts safe, in this shadowy glow.

FINDING OUR WAY HOME

Leaves flutter softly in the breeze,
Drifting to places unknown,
If fate allows, we'll meet once more,
Like a leaf from a tree, we'll find our way home.

Part Three

SEASONS OF CHANGE (20 POEMS)

Theme: Transformation, growth, and the cyclical nature of life.

Introduction: Life's rhythm mirrors the seasons—change is inevitable, beautiful, and often bittersweet.

CYCLES OF BECOMING

Beneath the frost, a seed takes root,
Silent whispers in the earth's pursuit.
Spring stirs softly with tender glow,
Turning the barren to life's warm show.
Summer bursts in colors bright,
Growth unfolds in the warmth of light.
Autumn whispers with a quiet grace,
Reminding us of time's gentle trace.
Winter comes, a peaceful pause,
Making way for the next new cause.

WHISPERS OF SPRING'S PASSAGE

Wind and rain see off the departing spring,
Gentle streams awaken, and swallows take wing.
Blossoms retreat, their petals adrift,
Time's quiet hands give the seasons a shift.
Flying snow welcomes the coming spring,
With whispers of warmth, new life they bring.
Morning sun dances on a glistening stream,
Nature unfolds like a painter's bright dream.
Each day, a story of change and serene.

TURNING LEAVES

The trees teach us best—
how to let go with grace.
Their colors fade,
but the beauty lingers
long after the fall.

THE SEEDLING

You buried me,
but I was a seed.
Through the darkness,
I stretched toward the sun,
reaching for the life
you thought I'd lost.

RAIN IN AUGUST

Unexpected storms
in summer's heat–
a reminder
that even in growth,
there is upheaval.

COCOON

Wrapped tight in silence,
I wait.
The world sees stillness,
but inside,
wings are forming.

WINTER'S END

The frost cracks,
and the earth softens.
Roots stir beneath the surface,
and the first brave shoots
reach for the light.

RIPPLE EFFECT

*A single pebble
dropped in still water—
the smallest change
creates endless waves.*

THE SCARS THAT BLOOM

These scars,
once jagged and raw,
have softened over time.
Now, wildflowers bloom
where the pain once was.

AUTUMN FAREWELL

*The wind carries away
the last of the leaves.
Bare branches stretch skyward–
not in despair,
but in readiness.*

SPIRAL PATH

Growth is not a straight line.
We circle back
to old lessons,
each time deeper,
each time wiser.

THE UNFINISHED PAINTING

Life is a canvas,
never truly complete.
Each brushstroke builds
on what came before,
creating a masterpiece
only change can make.

THE RIVER KNOWS

The river flows forward,
never clinging to its banks.
It carries the past gently,
but its heart beats
for the journey ahead.

After the wildfire,
new shoots emerge.
They are fragile,
but fierce—
proof that life begins again.

A WIND THROUGH THE GRASS

Change comes softly,
like a breeze
through an open field.
You don't see it happen,
but the landscape
is never the same.

THE EMPTY GARDEN

The garden sleeps,
its blooming long gone.
But even now,
its roots hum with life,
waiting for the sun's return

NIGHT BECOMES MORNING

Every night
whispers a promise-
that the sun will rise
and bring with it
a new beginning.

THE CHRYSALIS CRACKS

It hurts to break free.
But the cracks in the chrysalis
are where the light enters,
and where wings are born.

ETERNAL SPRING

Though winter will come again,
it cannot stay.
Spring waits patiently,
its blooms hidden,
its promise unbroken.

FULL CIRCLE

The cycle completes,
only to begin again.
Each ending,
a doorway;
each loss,
a seed for something new.

Part Four

RAYS OF LIGHT (20 POEMS)

Theme: Hope, resilience, and finding strength amidst adversity.

Introduction: Even in the darkest moments, light can find its way in, guiding us toward hope and new beginnings.

MORNING BREAKS

The night seemed endless,
but dawn crept in-
a golden thread
pulling me back to life.

THE CANDLE'S GLOW

Even a small flame
can pierce the blackest night.
Its warmth whispers:
you are not alone.

RESILIENCE

They said the storm
would break me.
But I am the oak—
bent, battered,
but still standing.

CRACKS OF GOLD

The cracks in me
are where the light enters,
turning my fractures
into radiant veins of gold.

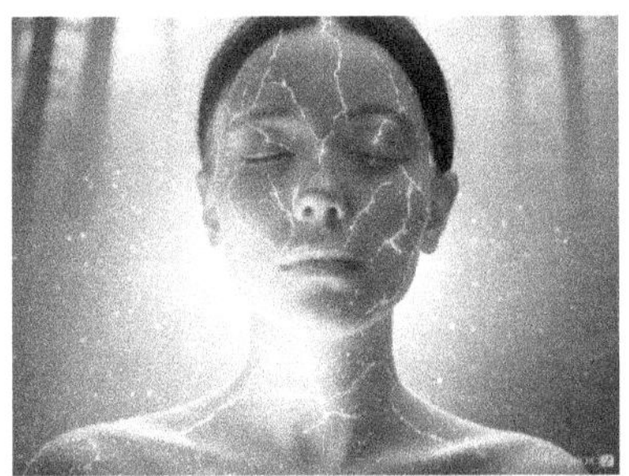

THE BRIDGE

The chasm seemed too wide,
but step by step,
I built a bridge of courage–
and crossed into the light.

When I thought I had nothing left,
I found wings
hidden beneath my scars,
ready to lift me.

THE QUIET FLAME

Hope doesn't shout;
it whispers.
A quiet flame,
steady against the wind.

AFTER THE RAIN

The storm passed,
and the earth smelled new.
Under the gray skies,
a single bloom–
proof that beauty persists.

LIGHTHOUSE

The waters raged,
but a steady light
on the horizon
showed me the way home.

A NEW DAWN

I feared the sun
would never rise again.
But here it is,
casting shadows behind me,
warming my face.

BLOOM AGAIN

They told me I was withered,
a garden long abandoned.
But with time,
I found the courage
to bloom again.

FOOTPRINTS

I thought I was alone
until I looked back
and saw the footprints
of everyone who walked with me
through the storm.

THE LIGHT WITHIN

I searched for the light
in others,
until I found it
shining quietly within myself.

THE FIRST STEP

The mountain loomed,
a shadow of doubt.
But I took one step,
then another–
and soon,
I was climbing.

ANCHORED

The waves tried to pull me under,
but I found my anchor—
buried deep in the strength
I didn't know I had.

SILVER LININGS

The clouds were heavy,
but through their edges,
a silver glow
reminded me
that storms don't last forever.

PHOENIX RISING

I thought I was ashes,
but within the dust
was a spark.
I rose from the flames,
reborn.

WINDOW OF HOPE

I opened the window,
and sunlight spilled in.
Even after the longest winter,
spring waits patiently
to return.

ENDLESS HORIZON

The horizon stretches on—
an open invitation.
Though the road winds,
I walk forward,
chasing the endless light.

BENEATH THE STARS

The vast expanse may feel so wide,
But stars above are by your side.
A quiet proof that through the years,
The light will guide you past your fears.

Part Five

REFLECTIONS OF THE SOUL (21 POEMS)

Theme: Introspection, inner peace, and spiritual musings.

Introduction: Quiet moments of self-awareness, finding beauty within, and connecting to something greater

FLEETING LIGHT

Ask the setting sun,
Why do you fade after you've shone?
How many joys and sorrows have you known?
For whom do you glow, and for whom do you go?
Can you stay and light my solitude just once?

QUIETUDE

In the stillness, a whisper calls,
A murmur soft, beyond the walls.
I sit, I wait, I let it be-
The peace that comes, so quietly.
In moments still, the soul does soar,
Not seeking more, but longing for.

MIRROR OF THE HEART

I gaze within the depths unknown,
A mirrored pool where truth is sown.
What reflections lie beneath my skin?
A light within, where dark has been.
In every crack, a piece of me-
A puzzle, whole, yet set free.

THE SPACE BETWEEN

Not in the noise, not in the haste,
But in the pause, the perfect space,
Where thought is still, and heart is clear,
Where presence dwells, and time stands near.
In quiet breath, I find my truth–
The space between is what is youth.

BENEATH THE SURFACE

There is a river deep inside,
Where currents flow, but none collide.
It moves in silence, full of grace,
A sacred realm, a quiet place.
Beneath the surface, calm and pure,
The soul's true form, forever sure.

THE SACRED PAUSE

Before the dawn, before the light,
I sit in stillness, pure delight.
No need to speak, no need to seek,
For in this moment, I am free.
The sacred pause, a breath divine,
Where soul and silence intertwine.

THE ETERNAL FLAME

A flicker small, a fire bright,
Within my chest, a sacred light.
It burns not with a hunger's grace,
But with a warmth, a soft embrace.
In darkness deep, it does remain,
The eternal flame, a soul's refrain.

A PLACE OF SOLITUDE

In solitude, I find my home,
No need for noise, no need to roam.
I close my eyes, I close my mind,
And leave the world far behind.
The peace I seek, the peace I know,
Is found in silence, soft and slow.

FRAGMENTS OF STILLNESS

The world is loud, a clamor strong,
But in my heart, a gentle song.
In fragments small, I find my peace,
A quiet song that will not cease.
The stillness calls, I heed its voice,
In silence, I rejoice.

ECHOES OF THE SOUL

An echo calls from deep within,
A voice of truth, where love begins.
It whispers softly, clear and true,
A melody for me and you.
In every beat, in every rhyme,
Echoes of the soul transcend time.

THE MIRROR OF THE SKY

Look to the sky, so vast, so wide,
A mirror for the soul inside.
The clouds may shift, the stars may fade,
But in its depths, my peace is made.
I see myself, I see the whole,
Reflected in the endless soul.

FLOW OF GRACE

In every breath, in every thought,
A river flows, a peace is sought.
It winds and bends, yet never strays,
A quiet stream through endless days.
In the flow, I find my grace,
A sacred rhythm, time and space.

SILENT PRAYER

A prayer unspoken, soft and pure,
Not of words, but of the heart's allure.
It speaks in silence, deep and still,
A quiet wish, a steadfast will.
In stillness, I am drawn to see
The divine within, eternally.

THE JOURNEY INWARD

A path unseen, a road unknown,
Yet, in my heart, I find my home.
The journey inward, dark and bright,
A quest for peace, a search for light.
In every step, I learn to be,
The soul that's always been set free.

STILL WATERS

The waters calm, the sky is clear,
The quite deep, the soul draws near.
A sacred space, untouched by time,
Where silence reigns, and all aligns.
In stillness, I have come to see
The deepest peace resides in me.

IN THE QUIET OF NIGHT

The stars above, the moon aglow,
The world asleep, a gentle flow.
In quiet night, I find my soul,
A place of peace, a quiet goal.
Here in the dark, I'm free to dream,
A silent truth, a steady stream.

A BREATH OF LIFE

In every breath, the world is born,
A sacred pulse, a love reborn.
I breathe in deep; I breathe out slow,
In every moment, life does flow.
A breath of peace, a breath of grace,
I find myself in this embrace.

THE DIVINE WITHIN

Not far away, not in the sky,
But deep inside, the truth does lie.
The divine is found in quiet eyes,
In moments still, beneath the skies.
I search not high, I search not wide,
For God is here, within, inside.

PEACE OF THE EARTH

The earth beneath, the sky above,
A sacred dance, a song of love.
In quiet earth, my roots run deep,
A peace that calls, a love I keep.
The earth and I, we share this space,
In gentle grace, we find our place.

SOUL'S REFLECTION

A mirror held, a soul revealed,
In quiet depths, my truth is healed.
Not in the rush, not in the race,
But in the calm, I find my place.
The soul reflects the light within,
A gentle glow, a place to begin.

EMBRACING SILENCE

I embrace the silence, warm and wide,
A sacred friend, a place to hide.
In quiet moments, I am whole,
The peace I seek, a quiet soul.
No words, no noise, just pure release,
In silence, I find endless peace.